The Power Within Me:
A Keep Rising! Girls' Guide to Loving Herself

The Power Within Me:
A Keep Rising! Girls' Guide to Loving Herself

Venus Alexandria Ferguson, M.Div.

COPYRIGHT

Keep Rising! Media Group
816 Brawley School Road, Suite D.
Mooresville, N.C. 28117

The Power Within Me:
A Keep Rising! Girls' Guide to Loving Herself
copyright 2016

All rights reserved. No part of this book may be reproduced in any form without prior consent of the publisher.

For more information, email
VenusAlexandria@KeepRisingSummit.com

ISBN: 978-0-692-60718-3

DEDICATION

This book is dedicated to my Lord and Savior, Jesus Christ, for giving me the strength and insight to answer the call.

To my mother, Sara Ferguson-Wagoner, you helped me develop the confidence that I have today.

INTRODUCTION

I wrote this book with you in mind. I know how hard it is to be a young lady, and it is my goal to help you realize that you are a beautiful and ambitious girl.

I want to help you increase your confidence so that you can be a positive influence in the world and among your friends. You are beautifully and wonderfully made with the ability to some day impact the world. My dearest Keep Rising! Girl, it is my hope that it becomes easier to overcome the challenges that you may face at home and in school.

This book is interactive and asks specific questions to help you better understand your journey through life. There are also *Keep Rising! Affirmations* throughout the book. Whenever you read an affirmation, I want you to repeat it aloud in the mirror. I hope that you will continue to set goals and dream big dreams because the reward for following your dreams awaits you.

Continue to press forward because you deserve the very best.

Keep Rising!

Keep Rising! Affirmation
I will follow my dreams.

Keep Rising! Affirmation
Surely the Lord is in this place.
Genesis 28:16

Keep Rising! Affirmation
You then my child, be strengthened
by grace that is in Christ Jesus.
2 Timothy 2:1

Good Morning, beautiful!
Daily Morning Affirmation

I am beautiful. I am unique. I am ambitious.
I am smart, and today will be a great day.

I promise myself to open-up to new opportunities
because one day I will change the world.

I will *Keep Rising!*

Good Night, gorgeous!
Daily Evening Affirmation

Today was a great day, no matter what may have happened. I am so beautiful, and there is no one like me. I love my family, and I love myself. Tonight, I will say my prayers and rest on the promises of God.
I will *Keep Rising!*

Keep Rising! Affirmation
Surely the Lord is in this place.
Genesis 28:16

Keep Rising! Girls attending the 2014 Keep Rising! Empowerment Summit for Girls.

Section One
Defining My Beauty

Keep Rising! Affirmation
I am beautiful, and no one can tell me otherwise.

When I look in the mirror, I see a
beautiful Keep Rising! Girl looking back at me.
Venus Alexandria

My definition of beauty is: _____
_____
_____
_____
_____
_____
_____

After writing my definition, I feel beautiful: ___ Yes ___ No

The reason that I think I am beautiful or not is because: _____
_____
_____
_____
_____
_____
_____
_____
_____

I can change how I view myself by doing: _____
_____
_____
_____
_____
_____
_____
_____

I feel beautiful when: _____
_____
_____
_____
_____

_____
_____
_____

There are times when I don't feel beautiful because:
_____
_____
_____
_____
_____
_____
_____
_____

I think that other girls are beautiful when: _____
_____
_____
_____
_____
_____
_____
_____

Some girls don't believe that they are beautiful because: _____
_____
_____
_____
_____
_____
_____
_____

This is what I will do to start believing that I am beautiful: ____
_____
_____
_____
_____

_____
_____

I will help other girls believe that they are beautiful by: _____
_____
_____
_____
_____
_____
_____

Keep Rising! Affirmation
Beauty is not always about my beautiful face.
It is also about the beauty in my heart.

How beautiful you are my darling! Oh, how beautiful!
Song of Solomon 1:15

When I look in the mirror, I think that the most beautiful part of me is: _____

_____
_____
_____
_____
_____
_____

If I could list five unique attributes about myself, they would be: _____

_____
_____
_____
_____
_____
_____

I believe that those are unique qualities because: _____

_____
_____
_____
_____
_____
_____
_____
_____
_____
_____
_____
_____

Keep Rising! Affirmation
When I look in the mirror, I realize that
I am beautifully and wonderfully made.

I believe that all girls are unique and beautiful.
Venus Alexandria

I believe that my unique attributes make me beautiful because: _____
_____
_____
_____
_____
_____
_____
_____

The unique attributes that I would like to change are: _____
_____
_____
_____
_____
_____
_____
_____
_____

I want to change those things because: _____
_____
_____
_____
_____
_____
_____
_____
_____
_____
_____
_____
_____
_____
_____
_____

Keep Rising! Affirmation
I am a beautiful girl!

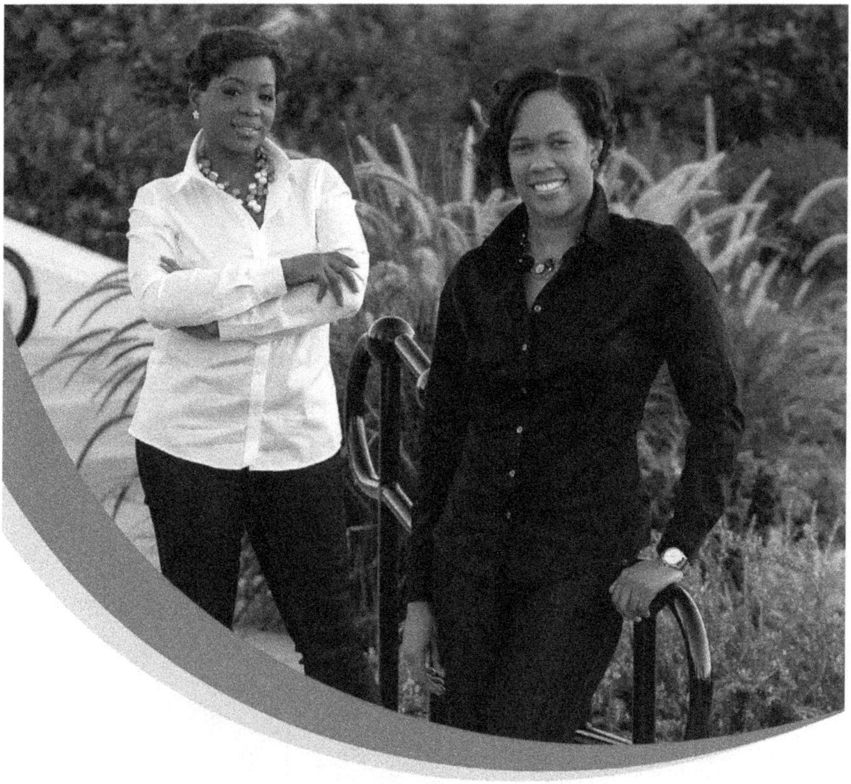

ALEX & ALSTON

DREAMERS SCHOLARSHIP FUND

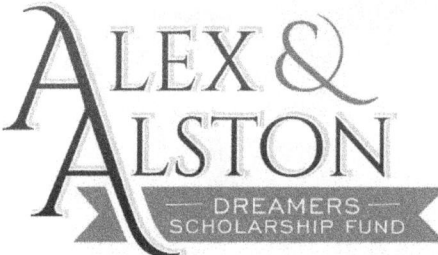

Venus Alexandria Ferguson- *Bachelor of Arts in Mass Communications from Winston-Salem State University | Master's in Divinity from Hood Theological Seminary*

Tracy Alston- *Bachelor of Arts degree in Sociology from Wake Forest University | Dual Master's degree in Community Agency Counseling with School Licensure from Lenoir-Rhyne University | Licensed Professional Counselor | Board Certified Neurotherapist*

Alex & Alston Dreamers Scholarship Fund

Empowering. Inspiring. Making dreams a reality.

For more information on how your high school senior can apply for the scholarship visit, *www.keeprisingsummit.com*

Section Two
I Have Feelings, Too.

Keep Rising! Affirmation
If I stand for what I believe in, I will change lives.

I believe that all girls should have a foundation that is created with joy and love. I also believe that girl's can do anything that they set their minds to do. It's all about girl power.
Venus Alexandria

To me, girl power means: _____
_____
_____
_____
_____
_____
_____
_____

One day, I want to change lives by doing: _____
_____
_____
_____
_____
_____
_____
_____

One day, I aspire to do: _____
_____
_____
_____
_____
_____
_____
_____

This is how I aspire to do those things: _____
_____
_____
_____
_____

Keep Rising! Affirmation
I will develop a plan that will impact lives.

Keep Rising! Affirmation
I am a child of God, therefore, I am blessed.

Praise you because I am fearfully and wonderfully made; your works are wonderful.
Psalm 139:14

I am wonderfully made because: _____
_____
_____
_____
_____
_____
_____
_____

This is what God means to me: _____
_____
_____
_____
_____
_____
_____
_____

I believe that God loves me because: _____
_____
_____
_____
_____
_____
_____
_____

I am blessed because: _____
_____
_____
_____
_____
_____
_____
_____

This is how I would describe my overall feelings about myself:

_____
_____
_____
_____
_____
_____
_____

I feel that way about myself because: _____

_____
_____
_____
_____
_____
_____
_____

I believe that God created me to do: _____

_____
_____
_____
_____
_____
_____
_____

I believe that God created me to be: _____

_____
_____
_____
_____
_____
_____
_____
_____

Keep Rising! Affirmation
I will pursue my education.

Education gives you confidence and choices.
Venus Alexandria

I will continue to pursue my education because: _____

_____
_____
_____
_____
_____
_____
_____

My goals for my education are: _____

_____
_____
_____
_____
_____
_____
_____

When I grow up, I want to be: _____

_____
_____
_____
_____
_____
_____
_____

The reason that I want to be a _____ is because:

_____
_____
_____
_____
_____
_____
_____

The challenges that could possibly keep me from pursuing my education are: _____

_____
_____
_____
_____
_____
_____
_____

This is how I can overcome those challenges:

_____
_____
_____
_____
_____
_____
_____
_____

I will encourage my friends to pursue their education because:

_____
_____
_____
_____
_____
_____
_____
_____
_____
_____
_____
_____
_____
_____
_____
_____

***Keep Rising!* Affirmation**
I promise myself to always set goals.

*But you, take courage! Do not let your
hands be weak, for your work shall be rewarded.
2 Chronicles 15:7*

I promise myself to set goals because: _____
_____
_____
_____
_____
_____
_____

These are the goals that I want to accomplish in the next month: _____
_____
_____
_____
_____
_____
_____

These are the goals that I want to accomplish in the next year:
_____
_____
_____
_____
_____
_____
_____

This is why I want to accomplish those goals: _____
_____
_____
_____
_____
_____
_____

With my best imaginative ability I will describe one of my future accomplishments, and how it will make me feel once it is accomplished: _____

_____
_____
_____
_____
_____
_____
_____
_____
_____
_____
_____
_____
_____
_____
_____
_____
_____
_____
_____
_____
_____
_____
_____
_____
_____
_____
_____
_____
_____
_____
_____
_____
_____
_____
_____
_____
_____

Keep Rising! Affirmation
I will participate in the things that I enjoy.

Consider it pure joy, whenever you face trials of many kinds.
James 1:2

I've been hurt by people that I loved and this is how it made me feel: _____

_____
_____
_____
_____
_____
_____

This is how I was hurt: _____

_____
_____
_____
_____
_____
_____

I believe I was hurt by this person because: _____

_____
_____
_____
_____
_____
_____

I won't hurt anyone like I was hurt because: _____

_____
_____
_____
_____
_____
_____

It is my goal to handle the pain by doing: _____

Letting Go of the Pain
Venus Alexandria

I remember the day my mother and I left Florida. We left to discover a life that was full of hope and happiness. A life that did not punish us for loving hard, and a life that promised stability and peace.

I was six- years- old when we boarded that vessel of hope. All of our personal belongings were tucked away neatly in its belly tagged with hopes and dreams of something new and better. However, my hopes and dreams stood on the other side. My hopes and dreams were my daddy. He was the first man to walk away and break my heart. I remember looking at my daddy with tear-filled eyes from the window of the Greyhound bus and blowing him kisses.

At that moment, I vowed to never cry again. So when the tears ran down my face, they poured from my soul for my daddy. I cried for him because I hoped that he would regret what he did and would come back to make it better. That day my innocence was replaced with the knowledge that I would never return to the embrace of my daddy again.

As the bus pulled away, I could smell the fuel from its bowels, and I watched my daddy fade away in the smoke. It wasn't like the movies when the person you loved ran after you and begged you to stay. Instead, it was a bitter reality when I watched him turn and walk away and not look back.

I've come to realize that in my departure was an

awesome gift from God. In the relinquishing of my innocence came a gift of peace from above. That gift, forgiveness. I've learned to forgive my daddy and pray to the Creator to continue to forgive.

Think about the person that hurt you. Have you forgiven them? Now, it is your chance to embrace your feelings and forgive them for what they have done to you. No matter how old you are, you have feelings too.

Keep Rising!

Keep Rising! Affirmation
My heart is full of love.

Great peace have those who love your law, and nothing can make them stumble.
Psalm 119:165

Is there anyone in your life that you need to forgive in order to have more love in your heart? Who is that person and how will you forgive them? _____
_____
_____
_____
_____
_____
_____
_____

My heart is full of love because: _____
_____
_____
_____
_____
_____
_____
_____

I will always keep love in my heart because: _____
_____
_____
_____
_____
_____
_____
_____

The things that encourage me to love are: _____
_____
_____
_____
_____
_____

Keep Rising! Affirmation
My happiness matters, too.

These are the things that make me happy: _____

_____
_____
_____
_____
_____
_____
_____

I will continue to focus on the things that make me happy because: _____

_____
_____
_____
_____
_____
_____
_____
_____

These are the things that make me unhappy: _____

_____
_____
_____
_____
_____
_____
_____

Those things make me unhappy because: _____

_____
_____
_____
_____
_____
_____
_____
_____
_____

When adults don't respect my feelings it makes me feel: ____
_____
_____
_____
_____
_____
_____
_____

The things that adults do that make me feel that they are not listening to me are: _____
_____
_____
_____
_____
_____
_____
_____

When adults don't listen to me, this is how I feel: _____
_____
_____
_____
_____
_____
_____
_____

Section Three
I Will Believe in Myself

Keep Rising! Affirmation
No one can take away my ability to believe in myself.

Trust in the Lord with all your heart, and do not lean on your own understanding. In all your ways acknowledge him, and he will direct your path.
Proverbs 3:5-6

Believing in myself is important because: _____

_____
_____
_____
_____
_____
_____
_____
_____
_____
_____
_____
_____
_____
_____
_____
_____
_____
_____
_____
_____
_____
_____
_____
_____
_____
_____
_____
_____
_____
_____

Keep Rising! Affirmation
I promise to never stop believing in myself.

I will always believe in my dreams.
Venus Alexandria

It is important that I believe in my dreams because: _____
_____
_____
_____
_____
_____
_____
_____

If I believe in my dreams, anything can happen because: _____
_____
_____
_____
_____
_____
_____
_____

My dreams are special to me because: _____
_____
_____
_____
_____
_____
_____
_____

My dreams can change the world because: _____
_____
_____
_____
_____
_____
_____
_____

Keep Rising! Affirmation
The sky is the limit for me.

Now to him who is able to do immeasurably more than all we ask or imagine, according to his power that is within us.
Ephesians 6:20

Some things are out of my power, but not out of God's power. This is what I want to ask God for: _____

_____
_____
_____
_____
_____
_____
_____
_____
_____
_____
_____
_____
_____
_____
_____
_____
_____
_____
_____
_____
_____
_____
_____
_____
_____
_____
_____
_____
_____
_____

This is why I can accomplish anything that I trust in God for:

The sky is the limit for me because: _____
_____
_____
_____
_____
_____
_____
_____
_____
_____
_____
_____
_____
_____
_____
_____
_____
_____
_____
_____
_____
_____
_____
_____
_____
_____
_____
_____
_____
_____
_____
_____
_____
_____
_____
_____
_____
_____
_____
_____

Keep Rising! Affirmation
I am ambitious, beautiful and smart.

Facing Your Obstacles
Venus Alexandria

It was exactly 2:14 a.m. when my feet hit the floor in an attempt to rest my busy mind. As I walked around my bedroom in the dim light shining through the windows, I wondered why I was awake. I grabbed my notebook and pen, turned on the light and began to write on the blank canvas in my hand. I wanted my spirit to speak.

I thought back over the past week and remembered vividly my trials and triumphs. I remembered my victories, and I remembered my tests. I also remembered the times when I was afraid. During those moments what I remembered most were my silent talks with God.

I picked up my Bible, and I began reading the book of Job. The Bible describes Job as a rich man that was blameless and upright. Job was a man that feared God. In this book, the Bible also illustrates exactly how Job was tested. He was tested just like me and you.

I encourage you to read the book of Job either on your own or with a parent. Did you know, that at any age, you will face obstacles. God knows that through your tests you will come out victorious. That is why he allows you to be tested. As you go through the ups and downs in life remember that no matter how old you are, you can overcome your obstacles. Keep Rising!

Ambitious girls are the most beautiful!
Venus Alexandria

This is why I would define myself as ambitious: _____

_____
_____
_____
_____
_____
_____
_____

This is what makes me ambitious: _____

_____
_____
_____
_____
_____
_____
_____

Ambition starts when I take the first step in doing: _____

_____
_____
_____
_____
_____
_____
_____

Keep Rising! Affirmation
My talents and gifts are from above.

*Every good and perfect gift is from above, coming down from
the father of heavenly lights,
who does not change like shifting shadows.
James 1:17*

My unique gifts are: _____
_____
_____
_____
_____
_____
_____
_____

I will believe in myself when no one else does because: _____
_____
_____
_____
_____
_____
_____
_____

At times, it's hard for me to believe in myself because: _____
_____
_____
_____
_____
_____
_____
_____

This is how I can increase my confidence and always believe in myself by doing: _____
_____
_____
_____
_____

Keep Rising! Affirmation
I can overcome all obstacles.

*Therefore, prepare your minds for action; be self-controlled;
set your hope fully on the grace to
be given you when Jesus Christ is revealed.*
1 Peter 1:13

These are the obstacles that I am currently facing in school: __
_____
_____
_____
_____
_____
_____
_____

These are the obstacles that I am currently facing at home: __
_____
_____
_____
_____
_____
_____
_____

I can overcome these obstacles by doing the following: _____
_____
_____
_____
_____
_____
_____
_____

Keep Rising! Affirmation
My life is more important than making poor decisions.

*I have decided to make myself
proud and not make poor decisions.
Venus Alexandria*

I have made poor decisions and they are: _____
_____
_____
_____
_____
_____
_____
_____

I consider them as poor decisions because: _____
_____
_____
_____
_____
_____
_____
_____

Those poor decisions made me feel: _____
_____
_____
_____
_____
_____
_____
_____

This is what I will do to ensure that I don't make those poor decisions again: _____
_____
_____
_____
_____
_____
_____

Keep Rising! Affirmation
I promise to do my best and always be at my best.

In addition to all this, take up the shield of faith, with which you can extinguish all the flaming arrows of the evil one.
Ephesians 6:16

To me, faith means: _____
_____
_____
_____
_____
_____
_____
_____

I have faith in myself to do the following things: _____
_____
_____
_____
_____
_____
_____
_____

When I am at my best, these are the things that I can accomplish: _____
_____
_____
_____
_____
_____
_____
_____

When I am not at my best, I know because: _____
_____
_____
_____
_____
_____

At times, I am not at my best because: _____
_____
_____
_____
_____
_____
_____
_____

I know when I am not at my best because: _____
_____
_____
_____
_____
_____
_____
_____

I promise to be at my best because: _____
_____
_____
_____
_____
_____
_____
_____

Keep Rising! Affirmation
I am confident that I have the ability to follow my dreams.

Keep Rising! Affirmation
I have beautiful skin, I have gorgeous eyes and everything about me is phenomenal. I am a smart Keep Rising! Girl who is ambitious and smart. My goal is to impact the world. I will *Keep Rising!*

I will never let go of my dreams.
Venus Alexandria

I plan to impact the world by doing: _____

_____
_____
_____
_____
_____
_____
_____
_____
_____
_____
_____
_____
_____
_____
_____
_____
_____
_____
_____
_____
_____
_____
_____
_____
_____
_____
_____
_____
_____
_____

Section Four
Learning How to Express Myself

Being understood is important.
Venus Alexandria

I want my mom to understand: _____
_____
_____
_____
_____
_____
_____
_____
_____
_____
_____
_____
_____
_____
_____
_____
_____
_____
_____
_____
_____
_____
_____
_____
_____
_____
_____
_____
_____

I want my dad to understand: _____

Section Five
Setting Long- Term Goals

No matter your age, setting long-term goals are important.
Venus Alexandria

In the next three years, I want to accomplish: _____

_____
_____
_____
_____
_____
_____
_____
_____
_____
_____
_____
_____
_____
_____
_____
_____
_____
_____
_____
_____
_____
_____
_____
_____
_____
_____
_____
_____
_____
_____
_____
_____

In the next five years, I want to accomplish: _____
_____
_____
_____
_____
_____
_____
_____
_____
_____
_____
_____
_____
_____
_____
_____
_____
_____
_____
_____
_____
_____
_____
_____
_____
_____
_____
_____
_____
_____
_____
_____
_____
_____
_____
_____
_____

Section Six
Encouraging Myself

Write a letter to your older self that encourages you to set goals: _____

Keep Rising! Girls attending the 2015 Keep Rising! Empowerment Summit for Girls

Section Seven
I Will Share the Love

Keep Rising! Affirmation
I am amazing, and I will tell someone about how amazing they are because they have inspired me.

I will love from my heart.
Venus Alexandria

Now that you've completed the book, how has it impacted you and the way you feel about yourself?: _____
_____
_____
_____
_____
_____
_____
_____
_____
_____
_____

I encourage you to revisit your responses, so that you can continue to love who you see in the mirror.

Write a letter and mail it to someone in your life that has positively impacted you. You can write your letter to a parent, a sibling or a teacher.

Write a letter and mail it to Venus Alexandria, the book's author, and tell her how you've been impacted by this book. Once she receives your letter you will receive a personal letter written by the author addressed to you.

Connect with the Author

www.AlexandriaFerguson.com | www.KeepRisingSummit.com

Twitter: @AlexKeepRising | Instagram: @AlexKeepRising

Facebook: VenusAlexandriaFerguson

www.ingramcontent.com/pod-product-compliance
Lightning Source LLC
Chambersburg PA
CBHW032208040426
42449CB00005B/499